Diversity in religion, spirituality and culture is an unqualified good for humanity. Gandhi said in his time that 'The friendly study of other religions is the sacred duty of each one of us'. Now more than ever we need to become experts of the major traditions of spirituality and religion. To do so will allow our collective understanding to see the common ground we all stand on in our various faiths. Brent Hunter is a person with a mission to spread the acceptance of pluralism around the world. His little book, *The Rainbow Bridge*, is a gem reflecting rays of wisdom from all the traditions of the religions, pointing to the common ground among us. We must learn to be comfortable on this bridge because it is our future.

— Brother Wayne Teasdale, Ph.D., author of *The Mystic Heart: Discovering a Universal Spirituality in the World's Religions*

i

From the beginning of time all we've ever wanted is to love and be loved, and from the beginning of time all we've ever done on this planet is make it nearly impossible to experience our highest desire. That is because we have imagined in our illusions that one of us is somehow better than another. This idea of "betterness" has created divisions between religions, between cultures, between people and between nations. The idea is also a false thought, directly contradicting the greatest teaching of all religions in the world which, put into one sentence, reduces itself to a simple truth: We are all one. *The Rainbow Bridge*, a wonderful little treasure conceived by Brent Hunter, is a demonstration of that truth that you can hold in your hand. Once held in your hand, you will hold it in your heart as well and it will illumine your soul.

— Neale Donald Walsh, New York Times Bestselling author of the five-book series *Conversations With God* (Books 1, 2 and 3), *Friendship With God* and *Communion With God*

This profound little gem is packed with a deep well of insights and wisdom. Communicating in a heartfelt way, with a clear desire to unify humanity, Brent Hunter gives us a roadmap to the conscious evolution of humanity. A book to carry in your pocket, consult often and give away to all those you care about.

— Elisabet Sahtouris, Ph.D., author of
EarthDance

The Rainbow Bridge is soul food, a bit of nourishment for the Spirit that can be read over and over again. It is a little book but packs quite a wallop.

— John Renesch, author of *Getting to the Better Future: A Matter of Conscious Choosing*

Here is a potent selection of Life-Charging thoughts.

— Jean Houston, Ph.D., New York Times Bestselling author of 26 books including *Jump Time* and *A Mythic Life*

The Rainbow Bridge

Universal Book of
Living, Dying and Dreaming

Collector's Edition

Spirit Rising Productions

ISBN 978-0-9979777-5-2
(Paperback Collector's Edition)

Republished on September 11, 2018
Text last updated on November 6, 2018

The symbols on the front cover are from the following major world religions, starting at the top center and moving clockwise in alphabetical order to reduce any perception of bias or preference: Bahá'ísm, Buddhism, Christianity, Hinduism, Islam, Jainism, Judaism, Native Spirituality, Sikhism, Taoism, Wicca and Zoroastrianism.

Cover design by Aldo Delgado (AldoDelgado.com)

The Rainbow Bridge

Universal Book of
Living, Dying and Dreaming

Collector's Edition

Brent N. Hunter

Spirit Rising Productions
Los Angeles, California

Contents

*"Build a bridge before
the river swells."*

— Thangtong Gyalpo

Dedication

To my dear mom, Isçe Güner Gökçen Hunter, and dad Jack Nathan Hunter. May you both always rest in peace.

To my beloved wife Dea, your boundless love, support, partnership, and ceaseless inspiration are priceless. You are a precious treasure to me and to the world, and I appreciate you beyond the ability of words to express.

To children and people of young spirit, to whom the future truly belongs.

"Those who know, do not speak; those who speak do not know."

— Tao Te Ching

With this in mind, I feel *something* needs to be said. Here are some of my thoughts and interpretations as of the date of the publication of this book.

"We are not human beings having a spiritual experience; we are spiritual beings having a human experience."

– Pierre Teilhard de Chardin

Who Is This Book For?

This book is for our brothers and sisters who are alive, dead, asleep, awake or anywhere in between.

This book is for men, women, children, youth, adults, and elder people. This book is for those who are seeking inner peace and world peace.

This book is for people from all walks of life in all corners of the world, for people of all races and all creeds, for people of all nations, all religions and all schools of thought.

This book is for all of the peoples of the world, for *WE ARE ALL ONE.*

The Rainbow Bridge

This book was written to facilitate the creation of a global culture of peace, harmony, wisdom, compassion, abundance and joyous living.

The primary intention of this book is to help create a bridge into this brave new world in a way that accepts, honors and respects all of the world's major religions, philosophies and schools of thought. It is a bridge that the rainbow-colored peoples of our planet are walking across that leads to greater heart-centered understanding and appreciation of one another worldwide.

We call this *The Rainbow Bridge*.

"Believe nothing, no matter where you have read it or who has said it, not even if I have said it, unless it agrees with your own reason and your own common sense."

— Author Unknown

Introduction

This book was not written by a religious scholar or expert. This book was written by a typical human being who has successfully emerged from several years of extremely challenging and intense experiences, relative to my prior experiences in my life.

During this period of challenging ordeals, I kept notes on what I considered to be of vital importance. This book contains all of the information, knowledge and wisdom that was of critical importance in navigating through those rough waters.

This book is designed to assist people who are going through any kind of challenge in life, anyone who is looking for more meaning, and for anyone who is looking for inspiration no matter who you are or where you live in the world. The principles in this book can be applied to experience success, happiness, peace, joy and bliss in your life.

In attempting to create my own way of understanding the world, I have tried to integrate as much spiritual knowledge from my own personal background and life experiences as possible. Born half Muslim, half Jewish and then raised as a Christian, this has not always been an easy task. Along the way, I have also integrated the wisdom of Buddhism, Hinduism, Taoism, Native American and Earth-based schools of thought. This book represents my current stage of integration of this information, knowledge and wisdom.

I offer this book as a gift to others who are seeking for more in their lives.

This book is meant to be simple, concise, direct and short. My intention is to summarize the information that I have learned in a way that is inclusive of all major world religions and schools of thought, with the goal of creating a truly inclusive book about peaceful, joyous, blissful and ecstatic living.

Books of Living and Dying and Books of the Dead

Many people have heard of *The Egyptian Book of the Dead* or *The Tibetan Book of the Dead*. It may come as a surprise to know that a large number of books have been written about living and dying, all with similar sounding names. Here are just a few, in alphabetical order:

- *The American Book of the Dead*
- *The Christian Book of the Dead (The Divine Comedy)*
- *The Egyptian Book of the Dead*
- *The Hindu Book of the Dead*
- *The Islamic Book of the Dead*
- *The Jewish Book of Living and Dying*

- *The Maya Book of the Dead: The Ceramic Codex*
- *The Pagan Book of Living and Dying*
- *The Tibetan Book of the Dead*

An Internet search will turn up a surprisingly large number of books with similar names; further exploration from various perspectives is encouraged.

The Rainbow Bridge is subtitled *Universal Book of Living, Dying and Dreaming* because it deals with the subjects of living, dying and dreaming in a non-dogmatic way that includes and honors all of the world's major religions and schools of thought.

So what's all of the fuss about life and death? Why are so many people talking about life and death – especially death?

Why is it considered to be so important to know all about death – to supposedly prepare ourselves and our loved ones for the afterlife? It's hard enough to live in this reality while focusing on life let alone learning anything about death. And therein lies the secret.

An open secret.

So while you read this short book, please expect things to be simple rather than complex. Expect to deal with paradoxes (mysterious and seemingly contradictory situations). Life and death are filled with mystery and paradox.

The wisdom in this introductory book is not new – it has been passed on throughout the ages by all of the world's major religious, spiritual and philosophical schools of thought. *The Rainbow Bridge* is my articulation of the wisdom of the ages and represents the common ground found within the world's major religions and wisdom traditions.

The concepts in this book may contain multiple layers of meaning. Read this book as many times as you wish, for your ability to understand and appreciate new interpretations will expand infinitely over time.

Although books, people, teachers and experience can provide a framework for understanding our lives, we always find our answers within. This is a consistent theme throughout this book.

Remember These Things

If you remember nothing else from this book, remember this **_wisdom_**:

1. "Reality" is not always as it appears; **_life is like a dream_**; an illusion; a hologram that is created by our individual and collective minds.

2. **_You are more than you think you are_**, and the power of your thoughts is astonishing. **_Anything is possible._**

3. The concepts in this book are **_simple_**, but **_not necessarily easy_**.

4. Treat all beings with **_compassion_**.

5. **_Love_**, **_Love_**, **_Love_**, **_Love_**, **_Love_**.

Universal Principles

The concepts in this book are universal and can be considered to be guidelines for living, dying, navigating through the dreamtime, traversing the labyrinth and for finding your way through the matrix of life.

Rather than being rigid rules, these universal principles can be utilized during your journey as ideas to be explored; things to keep in mind and as paradigms to guide you in the process of navigating through the experience that we so confidently call "reality".

"Never impose on others what you
would not choose for yourself."

— Confucius

The Golden Rule

Many of us grew up learning that The Golden Rule or ethic of reciprocity is "Do unto others as you would want them to do unto you."

An even more powerful and modern way of expressing this principle is "Do not do to others as you would not want done to yourself." Also known as the Platinum Rule, this is indeed a cardinal rule that applies to all people everywhere.

"The universe is dreaming
itself awake."

— Paul Levy

Life is a Dream

Things are not always as they appear; life is an illusion... life is very much like a dream.

Lucid dreaming is the experience of knowing you are dreaming while you are still dreaming at night. This not only allows you to effect the outcome of your dreams, but lucid dreaming also shows us that what we focus on (including what we fear) is what shows up in our dreams.

Just like we can become lucid and wake up when we're dreaming at night, *we can also become lucid during the daytime dream of life.*

As You Think, So It Is

You will manifest what you focus on. The expectations you have about the way something should happen have a direct impact on how it actually happens.

When scientists use instruments that measure waves, light appears to be a wave. When they use instruments that measure particles, light appears to be a particle. Life is the same way – we see what we expect to see; we experience what we think we will experience; we see what we believe we will see.

How do you know what you know?

Be careful what you think and believe;

As You Believe, So It Becomes

Life Can Be Difficult

Remember that although these concepts are simple, they are not always easy. Seek the support and assistance from other people of like mind. Friendship is important. Read Section 1 of *The Road Less Traveled* for an excellent treatment of discipline and "getting over" the difficulty of life. The basic premise is that once you accept that life is difficult, you won't be quite so upset when it is difficult. The very moment we accept this truth, the difficulty ceases to exist.

Although it can be extremely challenging, sometimes the best thing we can do for ourselves and for others is to accept what is so.

Life

Most of us know something about life... and most of us are also looking for more.

Many of us realize during our journey that the more we learn, the less we know. It is when we make this realization that true learning can occur, because we become more open to the totality of our experience... not to mention that we begin to learn things we never dreamed were possible.

Death

Most of us think we know something about death. However very often we don't really think about it happening to ourselves... and we certainly don't think of it happening to us any time soon. So we don't usually deal with the concept of death until it hits us.

However, the sooner we face our death the sooner we can become truly free. And the sooner we learn something about death, the sooner we can help those who are dying or help those who are caring for those who are dying.

Life After Death

Life follows death.

This is one of the most important concepts in this book. Once we recognize the truth in this and the relationship of this concept to us as individuals in this lifetime, we learn that death is actually an incredible illusion. Indeed, there is life after death.

The Path of Heart

Treat everyone with kindness, dignity, respect and honor. If it takes too much energy, then withdraw yourself from the situation so that your negative energies won't affect others; respect others' sacred space in public and non-public situations.

The Path of Heart has many implications, not the least of which means extending trust and giving others the benefit of the doubt as much as we possibly can. It's all about opening your heart ever more deeply to yourself and towards all other beings.

Be kind to all beings, whether or not you *think* they are living or sentient.

No Permanent Character Judgment

Do not judge others; view others as mirrors to learn more about yourself and to practice compassion.

Most of us constantly make judgments of one kind or another, especially about other people. It's best to not judge at all. However if we do judge, at least make temporary judgments. It's not helpful to permanently put a person into a certain category; they could have had a bad day, a bad month, a bad year or a bad decade (seriously!). Just like it's not useful when you are permanently labeled by someone else, it's not useful to do this to others.

Endless Connections

Everything in life is endlessly connected.

When we open our eyes to the wonder and beauty that surrounds us, we see that life is endlessly connected to everything else. Social scientists believe there are no more than six degrees of separation between any two people on the planet. It's similar with situations and events.

This is yet one more reason to not judge anyone or anything; in the grand scheme, the web of life is infinitely interconnected.

Love Your Neighbor

Love your neighbor, friend and foe alike. Love in this sense is not necessarily a feeling, it is a deliberate action.

There is acquaintance love, fraternal love, familial love, romantic love, sexual love and all sorts of combinations and permutations of love.

Open your heart. Love everyone, especially yourself.

It's not necessarily easy, but it is simple.

The rewards come not only to those we love but also to ourselves, for as we learn and practice love and compassion we gain levity, lightheartedness and inner peace.

Respect Your Elders

Respect, honor and revere your elders. We have a lot to learn from their experiences, from their wisdom and from their knowledge. We must never toss aside our elders such as is the predominant attitude in the United States.

Why do we do this to our elders? More than likely it is simply "because we can". This is a completely irresponsible way of using our vital resources. If you cannot see the value for their sake, do it for yourself, for you will be in their place in the future.

Respect our elders, they are our teachers and they are very important members of our human family.

Love and Compassion

Practice love and compassion for everyone you encounter, especially people that evoke fear or disdain. People are mirrors for us; if you look into the eyes of another person and see something you don't like, it's a sure sign that you have run into a limit to your acceptance of that person, as well as that part of yourself.

Unconditional love and compassion is not dependent on anything; it is freely given. As soon as there are strings or conditions, it serves the giver of love more than it does the intended receiver of love or compassion.

Practice unconditional love and compassion *for others* and *for yourself.*

Being of Service

The very act of being of service to others is empowering. Assisting others with heartfelt loving kindness connects us with the source of that which we all arise out of. It takes energy to be of service, it takes putting aside your ego and ultimately, going beyond the ego to a place where there is no separation. Service can be a path to liberation and freedom.

If I am not for myself,
Who will be for me?
If I am only myself,
What am I?
If not now,
When?

— Hillel

Karma is Cause & Effect

Karma is the law of cause and effect; actions have consequences.

Do not harm others because it will come back to you; "what goes around comes around".

If the concept of being nice isn't appealing, be nice for *yourself*, even if you don't want to be nice for the other person's sake. Your next life may be much sooner than you think it will be.

Love and Friendship

Whether you're in love romantically or whether you're enjoying loving time with friends or family, the benefits and results of love are many.

Love in all its forms is the golden key. Love supports you, love energizes you, love inspires you, love illuminates you, love expands you, love turns you on and of course love leads to ever greater states of peace, joy and bliss.

Love in its myriad forms is a portal that leads to a world of peace, happiness and ecstasy. The more we are able to love ourself and others, the more others can love us. The more we are loved, the easier it is for us to love others.

Love, Love, Love, Love, Love.

A Radiant Spark of Light

Even our smallest actions can make major differences in the lives of others. The power of a smile, the twinkling of an eye and the impact of any individual action may appear insignificant but it is not. The small things that we do benefit others and have untold ramifications for the generation of positive karma in your present and future lives, and in the lives of others.

Never underestimate the power of a single person to make a difference in the world.

Paradox and Mystery

Expect paradox and mystery on your journey; expect to go beyond your rational mind. Use your mind to go beyond your mind. Go beyond the dualistic world view of right/wrong, good/bad, positive/negative. There is a place that exists outside of these realms; this is referred to as going beyond the dualistic world or beyond the dual worlds.

This is very important.

The Greatest Mystery

Think out of the box; connect with something outside of yourself, whatever words you choose to use to describe the source or your concept of the source... the source of you, the source of your thoughts, the source of all that exists.

It appears that there are times when the source chooses to make itself known beyond the shadow of a doubt. During such times, if an individual attempts to deny its existence by the rational mind, tremendous suffering can ensue. We are one and the same as this never-ending, timeless, universal source of consciousness.

This is critical.

Find The Silver Lining

Challenges in life can be the very reason for growth and liberation. Alchemists refer to this as turning lead into gold in the heat of the fire.

One of the toughest challenges we face is to *find* the silver lining; this is an active process and is not always easy. Take this on either as an obligation or even better, a right that you have; you have a right to find that silver lining, it is always there for those who seek it out.

When all else fails, seek out the divinely comedic nature of life, for humor is very healing and can cure many ills.

The Power of Now

The only time we ever have is now; the past is gone and the future has not yet arrived. The present moment is all that we ever have. Learn to live in the present moment, it is precious. If you think about it for a while, you'll see the profound wisdom in this simple concept.

The time is now.

Through The Looking Glass

One of the most amazing experiences is to discover the non-dual world that transcends our typical experience of life. Returning to the "real world" matrix is not necessarily easy. One of the most difficult challenges is to return to the "real world" with the knowledge you have gained. Once you have stepped through the looking glass, there is no way to unlearn what you have learned. It is vital to bring the gifts of love, compassion, wisdom and understanding back to your everyday life and to share these gifts with others... to be "in the world but not of it".

Temet Nosce

Temet Nosce means "Know Thyself" in Latin. This is a very profound statement, for there are things that are completely and totally unknowable by anyone other than yourself. Seeking assistance and guidance from others is often very helpful and there are times when you must ultimately decide certain things for yourself no matter what anyone else says – no matter if it is your parents, clergy, so-called experts on various subject matters (especially psychologists and psychiatrists), gurus or anyone else. There are times when looking outside for guidance is actually detrimental to you – your center is always within you. Seek within to connect to your direct knowledge.

Standing Up

Remember that you cannot always please everyone and sometimes the very best thing you can do is to stand up, straighten your back, hold your head up high and meet your own needs.

The importance of this is shown to us every time we fly in an airplane. The flight attendants always tell passengers to put the oxygen mask on yourself *before* you put the masks on other people sitting next to you – including children and elders. Unless you take care of yourself, you won't be around to take care of anyone else.

Ask For What You Want

This sounds easy but sometimes the hard part is not asking for what we want but first knowing what we want. If we don't know what we truly want, it is difficult to ask for it. Sometimes the hardest part is to learn enough about ourself to know what we truly want... this comes from learning; this comes from self knowledge; this comes from discernment.

Once we are clear what we want from ourself, others and from situations, stand tall and ask for what you want.

Ask and You Shall Receive

Taking Responsibility

In times of severe stress, uncertainty and extreme doubt, it is easy to give up hope and to think that everything that is happening to you has nothing to do with you.

In almost all situations, it is more empowering and ultimately more beneficial to you to take full responsibility for your thoughts, feelings, actions and choices.

Dedication, Devotion and Commitment

Dedication, devotion and commitment to oneself, to other people, to work and to life itself can sometimes require deep faith and persistence. Sometimes things don't come easy but with dedication, devotion and commitment, the forces in the universe converge and deliver.

Commitment and dedication is especially important when you are looking for the support and/or participation of other people, for if you do not demonstrate serious levels of commitment and dedication, they may understandably lack confidence in you.

When you demonstrate commitment and devotion in any type of relationship, it should be obvious that the other person or persons will be much more likely to also show such dedication and commitment.

One definition of "insanity" is to do the same thing over and over and over again and expect the same result. A good way around this conundrum is to try new and different approaches, always keeping in mind the goal you have and not necessarily insisting that the one specific path to get to that goal is the only way to get there.

There are many ways to get past a fence – over, underneath, around or through.

Truth and Honesty

It is to you and others' benefit to be truthful, honest and genuine in your words and in your actions.

There are times when it is easier to not tell the truth or to be less than honest. It is during those times when telling the truth can come at a cost to ourselves. When we tell the truth regardless of the cost, it is ultimately empowering because we are doing what we know to be right.

Truth and honesty are the right thing to do, and are excellent policies to have in all areas of our lives.

Timing and Sequence

There are times when we are motivated to not do anything, to relax, to let things be and go with the flow. However, there are also times when we are motivated to be in action mode. When stepping into the mode of action, it is important to consider two things in particular to whatever it is that you are doing.

The first is the timing of your actions. This is somewhat self evident.

The second is the sequencing of your actions; sometimes this is easy to forget or to not think about.

Not "If", But "How"

When you are attempting to create or manifest something that you desire or want in life, it is helpful to act with a deep belief that you will in fact see the desired outcome.

Don't wonder *if* you will be able to do something – wonder *how* you will do it. Don't wonder *if* you will be able to do something – wonder *when* you will do it. Don't wonder *if* you will be able to do something – wonder *under what circumstances* it will happen.

Acting from a sense of knowing that you will manifest what you want increases the probability of actually attaining it, whatever it is.

Balance & Moderation

Seek balance and moderation in all areas of your life to move closer and closer toward true inner peace.

In some circumstances and situations, it's to your advantage to use not just moderation but extreme moderation.

Imbalances are not always easy to see... they can be our "blind spots".

Surrender

There are times in life when things don't turn out the way we wanted them to. There are times when it is clear that the outcome was out of our control and there is nothing else we can do. During such times, it is important to "surrender" to the situation. Indeed, sometimes it is the only choice we have. In such situations we can gracefully surrender to the situation as it is, or we can struggle and suffer, kicking and screaming along the way.

Although this is easier to say than to do, it's a very important concept to remember along the journey of life.

Meditation and Sitting

Sometimes the best thing you can do is to meditate, to "just sit" or to "just be". Sometimes just sitting and contemplating is deeply centering. There are thousands of ways to just sit, including a large number of different meditation techniques. *Just relax.*

Sometimes when we are sitting or not sitting, getting out of our heads and into our feelings is the best thing – and sometimes the only thing – we can do for ourselves in certain difficult periods of time.

Sitting can lead to surrender to acceptance and to deep inner peace.

Dynamics of the Ego

We hear all the time of people who have "big egos". We read that the ego is something to overcome, something to slay, something to get rid of. However I believe the best way to think about the ego is that it can be transformed. One of our goals is to transform the ego from being self- centered to being other-centered.

Seen in this light, it's not bad to have a transformed big ego because it makes us more effective at manifesting things that are for the benefit of others. Being centered on meeting the needs of others is another way of saying that we are being of service to others.

Expect Changes

Expect the unexpected and have no fear. Things change; be willing to release your grip, your control and your attachments.

There are very few guarantees in life. However death and change rank near the top, so it only makes sense to come to terms with the fact that life is not always permanent and that it can change. This is a very profound way for us to learn to live in the present moment and to experience the bliss and perfection that is already here.

Don't Take Things Personally

Sometimes things happen in life that have nothing whatsoever to do with us and yet we ascribe meaning to these situations as if it did have something to do with us. Sometimes we're at the grocery store and the clerk is rude to us and we get upset. The clerk could be going through a rough time in their life. Rather than thinking "how could they be so rude to me!", don't take it personally and just let the person have their bad day. When we don't take things personally, we can often see situations more clearly, more objectively and with less frustration.

Peaks and Valleys

Vital energy is often experienced in peaks and valleys. These peaks and valleys are a natural part of life.

Another way to describe these peaks is to say that vital energy shifts or is transformed at times. It is important to know that energy doesn't disappear, it just gets transformed into different forms of energy. When energy is not appearing in an abundant fashion, conservation can sometimes be helpful.

Choose your battles wisely, choose your career wisely and choose what you spend your time and energy on wisely.

The Darkness

Sometimes we have to wander in the empty valley in order to more fully appreciate the peaks. Sometimes we have to experience the horrible searing pain of darkness and suffering in order to more fully appreciate the light. Sometimes we have to enter the hot and dry desert in order to more fully appreciate the deliciousness of the oasis. Sometimes we have to taste bitterness in order to fully appreciate sweetness.

The dark is thus the catalyst that can facilitate a greater appreciation for the gift of light.

Moving On

Reactions and emotions such as fear, anger, jealousy, pride, etc. are all within your control. Other people can try to push your buttons but the buck stops with you when it comes to what you think, what you say and what you do. Don't expect this to be easy, because sometimes it's not... but it is always in your control. Although it might seem harsh, sometimes we have to "just get over it" when it comes to dealing with the circumstances and situations that arise in life.

Don't Panic!

There are times when the weight of the world seems heavy on our shoulders. Sometimes the discoveries we make and experiences we have are shocking, difficult and overwhelming. Sometimes we can become exhausted, overwhelmed and disoriented. Indeed, our very sense of reality can become challenged. This is exactly what happens when the mental, rational, intellectual mind is pushed beyond its limits.

During times such as these:

- Don't panic
- Don't have fear
- Breathe
- Seek out the support of others
- Trust the process

Breathe

Breathe! Seriously, sometimes it is incredibly helpful to just sit and take deep breaths. Focus on your center, find the spot within where the peace is, and breathe into that space. If you think you can't find any kind of inner peace, focus on where you think the peace is, where it could be or where you want it to be.

If all else fails, don't think about anything – just take deep breaths and feel the energy and life force coming into your body.

This is important.

Trust

Have trust and keep the faith no matter what you *think* is happening. Don't get hung up on differences between trust, faith, etc... the base concept is the same. Keep your mind and body and soul focused on whatever it is that you want.

No matter how long you feel like you have been struggling or suffering, keep the faith... there is light at the end of the tunnel. Don't lose the faith, otherwise YOU will be the cause of you letting go, not anyone else or anything else.

The section titled "Dedication, Devotion and Commitment" is important with respect to the issue of trust.

Let Go of Fear;
Become Fearless

As Franklyn D. Roosevelt once said, "the only thing we have to fear is fear itself". This is a true, profound and important statement.

Getting rid of our fear is not always easy. Seek out others who you can learn from, who support you, who empower you, who inspire you and who uplift you. Friendship is important in overcoming fear.

Focus on What
You Want

We manifest what we focus on. Therefore do not focus on what you fear, *focus on what you want*; focus on the future you want to create.

Acting "As If"

If you're not sure about your ability to do something, act "as if" something were already true – this is a very powerful way to achieve success.

This is related strongly to the section titled "Not If, But How".

The Power of Thought

Your thoughts are extremely powerful.
Your thoughts are the seed of physical
manifestation.

*Anything is possible with focused
attention and intention.*

Focus, Focus, Focus

Concentrate

Interpretation

Mastering interpretation is of great importance. Things that happen in our lives do not always have inherent meaning; we create meaning based on how we interpret the things that happen in our lives. It is helpful to make an effort to always use the most empowering and uplifting interpretation for yourself and others.

For example, if one knows that life's energy naturally comes in ebbs and flows, one is less likely to interpret the ebb and flow as something that we have brought upon ourselves.

This is very important and practice makes a big difference.

Perspective

One way to understand a difficult situation is to approach it from a different perspective. Often when we can view a situation from someone else's perspective (or a different perspective), we can see the situation in an entirely new way.

In order to arrive at the most inspiring, uplifting and empowering interpretation about any given situation, it is helpful to approach it from a different perspective. Try out different perspectives and you'll be amazed at what you can learn.

This is very important and practice makes a big difference.

Information & Wisdom

Our ability to understand our lives, our ability to form the most inspiring interpretations and our ability to have the most useful perspective is dependent upon the information, knowledge and wisdom that we have access to.

For those who are fortunate enough to have access to it, the Internet allows unparalleled access to information, knowledge and connections to other people worldwide.

Stay tuned in to what is happening on the Internet; the global brain is awakening in cyberspace. Information, knowledge and wisdom are there for those who seek it out.

Discernment

From Webster's Revised Unabridged Dictionary (1996):

Discernment \Dis*cern"ment\, n. The power or faculty of the mind by which it distinguishes one thing from another; power of viewing differences in objects, and their relations and tendencies; penetrative and discriminate mental vision; acuteness; sagacity; insight; as, the errors of youth often proceed from the want of discernment.

Some types of discernment come only through experience, over time and with knowledge of the self. What is discerned by you may not be discerned in the same way – or at all, by others. Look within to discern knowledge directly.

There is Always More

Sometimes we can have awakening or enlightenment experiences that significantly expand our consciousness. This can lead to the blissful experience of feeling like we are at one with the cosmos; where the inner becomes the outer; where the macrocosm becomes the microcosm, where above becomes below, etc. At that point we can feel like we know everything there is to know. This can be dangerous because we can have secondary and tertiary awakenings where we learn that there is more to learn. There is no end to consciousness. This realization can either be very daunting or it can give rise to tremendous inner peace if we stay in the present moment.

Follow Your Heart

We normally guide ourselves by using our rational mind. While the mind can be a powerful tool, when we are faced with difficult decisions it helps to remember that we have an entirely different faculty for helping us make decisions, our heart; our intuition. I believe that we can almost never make a wrong decision if we follow our hearts. We may make what we *think* are mistakes from time to time, but even these situations lead to learning, personal growth and a deeper sense of knowing who you are and what is important to you.

If you are ever in doubt whether to follow your mind or your heart, follow your heart for direct knowledge.

Music - The Universal Heartbeat

Music is a universal language that unites people from all walks of life, from all cultures, and in all corners of the world. Music soothes and heals heart, body, mind and soul. Music helps bring us to an inner space that is outside of time and space, and music brings us closer to peace, joy and bliss.

Music is the voice of all humanity, of whatever time or place. In its presence we are one.

– Charlotte Gray

Music washes away from the soul the dust of everyday life.

– Red Auerbach

Mystical Love

The way of love is the great way.

When we love, we want to love totally, completely. But when we love, loving a person or falling in love with God, the Absolute, our love fails us. We say, "I will love you forever". How quickly we get caught up in other events, other interests. Non-love is our ordinary state.

To learn the way of love means to train in eternal love, ceaselessly loving. To keep loving, like breathing itself – never being distracted from this involvement in love. Then we enter into a new state – then we experience mystical love. This is an entirely new state of human evolution.

– Venerable Lama Kunzang Rinpoche

Express Appreciation

Express gratitude and appreciation for what you *do* have. Don't take anything for granted.

If you feel that you're not getting everything you want in life, think of the things you don't get that you don't want. Seriously!

Listen to Others

Learn to listen, for then you will be heard.

If we are speaking, we are not listening or learning anything to add to our sum of knowledge. This is why the first step to effective listening is to stop talking!

– Ken Fracaro

The most basic of all human needs is the need to understand and be understood. The best way to understand people is to listen to them.

– Ralph Nichols

Share With Others

Learn to give, for then you will receive.

Very often, giving or sharing what we ourselves have been denied or what we have little of can be very healing. What you give will be returned to you at least tenfold.

Give and share what you can, when you can, while you can.

Live and Let Live

Learn to allow, for then you will be free.

As we allow others to "just be", we learn how to appreciate them exactly as they are. To the extent we do this for others, inner appreciation for ourselves flourishes. As we let others have the freedom to be who they are, we gain the freedom to be who we are.

You don't have to agree with others in order to let them be; to let them live.

Notes on Synchronicity

Synchronicity is the occurrence of "meaningful coincidence"; the incidence of events that seem to be meaningfully related.

The more we are drawn into the dream of life, the more we become conscious of the incredible synchronicities that happen all around us almost constantly. To the extent that we understand what synchronicity is and make a point to be on the lookout for it in our lives, we will see and experience synchronicities with greater frequency and greater profundity. The experience of life becomes ever more magical, more blissful and more filled with awe and wonder.

Notes on Learning

One of the challenges along the way is to learn something really profound, because it can lull you into a sense of feeling like you know everything there is to know. Then, when you least expect it, you will get another lesson that teaches you that there is more.

Just like trying to find our way out of a labyrinth or a maze, sometimes we return to situations and lessons that we thought we already had mastered... and then we learn a new paradigm or a better way. Our ability to focus our mind, to focus our attention and to focus our intentions are good examples of lessons which we can return to again and again.

One final comment about learning. There are times in life when we feel that we are "in school". To the extent that you are hanging out with a group of people and you feel that you are "in school", this can be a good sign. It is important to note that there are many schools of thought and that exploration can sometimes add clarity to your learning and growing experiences.

The seminar of "life" on Earth is something we all share in common as fellow human beings – we're all in it together.

Putting It All Together

While reading this book you may have been frustrated at times because some of the concepts seem to contradict other concepts. Going within yourself to find the answers and "thinking out of the box" can be helpful in putting the pieces of the puzzle together.

Here is an example. Walking The Path of Heart calls for treating everyone you meet with love, dignity, honor and respect. Another concept we've discussed is standing up and meeting your own needs. Yet another concept we've discussed is being honest, truthful and genuine. How do all of these fit together? What if we meet someone we really don't like? Shouldn't we meet our own needs, be truthful, be authentic and let them know what we *really* think?

The key to answering this question is to know whose interests are being met when you make a decision or take an action. If you see or encounter someone that rubs you the wrong way and you still respect, honor and treat them well, you are meeting their needs and you are putting out positive energy in the world. In a small but definite way, you are making the world a better place. If you insist on telling that person how horrible they are and how they should change their ways, you are meeting your own needs. That person (no matter how right *or* wrong you are) will not be uplifted; they will experience negative energy. One way to get around this conundrum is to take yourself away from that person so that you won't be tempted to give them your negative energy... and then talk it over with your friends later to get it out of your system in a genuine way by telling your truth.

There are times in life when practicing the concepts such as the one described above takes more energy out of you than you have or than you want to give. Love is an active process that requires time and energy. It is important to take care of yourself and to meet your own needs. The only person that can truly know what decision to make in such situations is you.

Learning to strike a balance between meeting our own needs and meeting the needs of others can be a major life challenge and learning opportunity.

It can often be very helpful to read books, to see movies, to seek the advice and counsel of others and to see how other people are handling various situations in their life – but in the final analysis, all of our answers are within. Seek within, look inward to discern your own inner truth and don't stop until you experience inner peace, joy and bliss.

When all else fails, trust your intuition, follow your heart and follow your bliss.

Implications

After further contemplation, the implications of this information are profound if this wisdom, knowledge and information were to be understood and applied by more people on the planet.

I hope that this knowledge can be understood and integrated in all fields of endeavor, including business, politics, science, health, medicine, culture, spirituality, art, music and ecology.

There is a vast potential for improvement in the quality of life for all people on the planet. Together let's walk across The Rainbow Bridge that leads into an age of peace, joy, abundance and prosperity for all people everywhere.

A Living Book

Words are approximate and thus limited. One slight change in wording can lead to major changes in meaning. Communication is not an exact science.

Words are approximations to meanings and will never be completely sufficient to communicate completely. If we know this in advance, however, then we won't run into too much trouble because we know in advance that we can resolve misunderstandings by having further communication and discussion. Through further communication comes information and with new information comes evolution. Communication and open-minded discussion are critical to our evolution as individuals and as a World Community.

A companion web site for this book is being created to facilitate such an ongoing discussion.

The interactive online system will facilitate further discussion, learning and networking with respect to the concepts contained in this book – and many other subjects – with other people around the world from various cultures, schools of thought and walks of life. I also hope to have leading authors, teachers and lecturers available to answer questions, to provide classes and to help further explore the subjects in this book. An additional benefit will be the ability to network with other people of like mind, whatever your mind might be.

The Rainbow Bridge web site is located at therainbowbridge.tv .

Quotations

For Inspiration On
Your Journey

Brilliance

Our biggest fear is not that we are inadequate.

Our deepest fear is that we are powerful beyond measure. It is our light, not our darkness, that most frightens us.

We ask ourselves, who am I to be brilliant, or gorgeous or talented or fabulous? Actually, who are you NOT to be? You are a child of God. Playing small doesn't serve the world.

There's nothing enlightened about shrinking so that other people won't feel insecure around you.

Brilliance (continued)

We were born to make manifest the glory of God that is within us.

It's not just in some of us; it's in every one of us.

And as we let our own light shine, we unconsciously give other people permission to do the same.

As we are liberated from our own fear, our presence automatically liberates others.

– From *A Return to Love,* by Marianne Williamson

Child of The Universe

I am a child of the universe –

With the glitter of my life, I travel through black, velvet space, and the gates of time –

I am a star, awoken from its sleep, by the longing cries of mankind's dreams –

Dreams of harmony, love and a child of the universe...

– From *A Child of the Universe*, by Ralph-Armand Beck (DJ Taucher)

Persistence

Nothing in the world can take the place of persistence.

Talent will not; nothing is more common than unsuccessful men with talent.

Genius will not; unrewarded genius is almost a proverb.

Education will not; the world is full of educated derelicts.

Persistence and determination alone are omnipotent.

– Calvin Coolidge

Perseverance

He failed in business in 1831.

He was defeated for State Legislator in 1832.

He tried another business in 1833. It failed.

His fiancee died in 1835.

He had a nervous breakdown in 1836.

In 1838 he ran for Congress and was defeated.

He tried again in 1839 and was defeated again.

Perseverance (continued)

He tried running for the Senate and lost.

The next year he ran for Vice President and lost.

In 1859 he ran for the Senate again and was defeated.

In 1860, the man who signed his name

Abe Lincoln was elected

President of the United States.

The Serenity Prayer

God grant me the serenity to accept the things I cannot change;

Courage to change the things I can; and the wisdom to know the difference.

– Dr. Reinhold Niebuhr/Friedrich Oetinger

Wishes Come True

"You are never given a wish without also being given the power to make it true. You may have to work for it, however."

– From *Illusions*,
by Richard Bach

What is Your Dream?

"Do you have a dream? If not, create one. Dreams are what keep us going."

– From *The Pieces of Our Puzzle*, by
Brent Hunter

Bliss

"Follow your bliss."

– Joseph Campbell

Excellence vs. Perfection

"Perfection is being right.
Excellence is willing to be wrong.

Perfection is fear.
Excellence is taking a risk.

Perfection is anger and frustration.
Excellence is powerful.

Perfection is control.
Excellence is spontaneous.

Perfection is judgment.
Excellence is accepting.

Perfection is taking.
Excellence is giving.

Perfection is doubt.
Excellence is confidence.

Excellence vs. Perfection

(continued)

Perfection is pressure.
Excellence is natural.

Perfection is the destination.
Excellence is the journey."

– From *You're the Greatest*,
Francis X. Maguire

The Time Is Now

"We are the people the world has been waiting for... and now is the time to act as one."

– Adapted from A Message From
The Hopi Elders

Conflict and Harmony

"The purpose of conflict is
to restore harmony."

– Brent N. Hunter

The Rainbow Bridge Vision

- A rainbow-colored tribe of people from all walks of life in all corners of the world comes together in the spirit of creating more cooperation, harmony, understanding and happiness worldwide.

- A grassroots global phenomenon is created. A massive network of networks mobilizes to take part in conversations and dialogues that lead to greater understanding and appreciation of each other worldwide.

- ***The Rainbow Bridge*** book shows the common ground in all religions and receives distribution worldwide. The book is translated into many different languages and formats.

- To help our brothers and sisters in need, a large number of corporate, organizational and individual sponsors purchase copies of *The Rainbow Bridge* for free distribution at orphanages, child care centers, foster care homes, homeless shelters, hospices, retirement homes, community mental health centers, juvenile detention centers, rehabilitation centers and prisons.

- A large online presence is created to facilitate communication, dialogues and greater understanding of other peoples, cultures and ways of life worldwide. It is literally a portal to a new world.

- To the astonishment of many people, the world enters an unprecedented era of peace, harmony and abundance.

2001 Acknowledgements

My deepest heartfelt thanks, appreciation and gratitude go to the following people who loved, supported and/or stood by me during the most trying of times (in alphabetical order by last name): Jon Appleton, Denise Attewell, Donna Attewell, Tolly Burkan, Tony Coleman, Mark Comings, Richard Curtis, Steven Desdier, Lisa Devenish, Carlin Diamond, George White Eagle, Peter Ellison, Gary Wayne Farris, Ron Fleisher, Liz Freeman, John Gunderson, Chad Hamilton, Jack Hunter, Nicole Hunter, Lama Kunga Rinpoche, Lama Kunzang Rinpoche, Jayne Landon, Elizabeth and Dick Lepre, Paul Levy, Richard Maldonado, Drew Maris, Elise Mercado, Ari and Monica Pärnänen, Debra Pearlstein, John Renesch, Nirmalpal Singh Sachdev, Brian Silva, David Turk, Karen Rae Wilson, Reinhold Ziegler, Park Employees, Park Volunteers, Park Advisors, Park Members and the entire cosmic tribe worldwide. Thank you for your support, never-ending love and unfailing belief in me through thick and thin.

I also give special thanks to all of my brothers and sisters worldwide who came before me, for we truly stand on the shoulders of the giants who have come before us.

Grateful acknowledgement is made to Marianne Williamson for permission to reprint her inspiring quote in the back of the book, to DJ Taucher/Ralph-Armand Beck for permission to reprint the awesome lyrics to "A Child of the Universe", to Paul Levy to print his awakening quotation "the universe is dreaming itself awake" and to Venerable Lama Kunzang Rinpoche for his beautiful writing on Mystical Love.

About The Author

With twelve active professional certifications in project management, knowledge management, change management and agile methodologies, Brent Hunter is a senior IT executive consultant, entrepreneur, author, producer and executive producer, former psychotherapist and National Certified Counselor. Hunter is also a social media pioneer as the founder of the first intentional World Community in cyberspace called "The Park," with more than 700,000 members in 190 countries worldwide.

Brent is part Muslim and part Jewish, and was brought up as a Christian. He currently studies and lives by an integrated set of life principles including Bahai'i, Buddhist, Christian, Confucian, Earth-based, Hindu, Islamic, Jewish, Native American/Indigenous, Sikh, and Taoist traditions. Brent believes that all paths are divine and must be equally respected in order for the world to become a significantly better place for all of our brothers and sisters worldwide.

Brent received a B.S. in Math and Computer Science from Clarkson University, an M.S. in Counseling and Human Relations from Villanova University, and the equivalent of an M.S. in Information Systems after he graduated from the General Electric Company's fast-track Information Systems Management Program.

Brent is an Eagle Scout, a graduate of the U.S. Army Airborne School, and is involved with a number of global civic organizations, including a past position in the United Nations Association of the U.S. as the Vice President of Communications in the Northern California Division. He is also the author of *The Power of KM: Harnessing the Extraordinary Value of Knowledge Management*, *The Pieces of Our Puzzle: A Multi-Faceted Approach to Personal Success and Well Being*, *Nuggets of Wisdom: Quotes to Ponder and Inspire*, *More Nuggets of Wisdom: Quotes to Ponder and Inspire*, and the upcoming *The Park Odyssey*.

After being born in Brooklyn, NY and living in Upstate New York, Philadelphia, Chicago and San Francisco, Brent currently lives, plays, and works in Los Angeles, CA with his beloved wife Dea, German Shorthaired Pointer/Chocolate Lab Kenai and North American Sphynxes Bindi and Bambi.

Afterword

The edited book you are reading was originally published in 2001 as the first edition of *The Rainbow Bridge: Universal Book of Living, Dying and Dreaming*. My mission was to illuminate the common ground in the world's major wisdom traditions in the most concise way possible. The second edition was translated into 24 languages by a team of international volunteers, to whom I am eternally grateful. As a result of using Craigslist to locate volunteers, The Rainbow Bridge was featured in the movie "24 Hours on Craigslist."

The significantly expanded book is now in its 4th edition and is titled *The Rainbow Bridge: Bridge to Inner Peace and to World Peace*. I am humbled to share that as of 2018, it has received 22 literary awards and has been endorsed by H.H. the 14th Dalai Lama, New York Times best-selling authors, doctors, attorneys, Ambassadors, astronauts, Olympians, an Academy Award-winning actor and a growing chorus of global luminaries.

Since the 4th edition of The Rainbow Bridge was published in 2014, I published my first business book, about Knowledge Management (KM). Since KM includes the realm of wisdom, I refer to KM as the doorway to greater wisdom and heart in business. The name of that book is *The Power of KM: Harnessing the Extraordinary Value of Knowledge Management*. The connection between that book and this one is *The Rainbow Bridge* contains universal wisdom. Wisdom is at the apex of the Wisdom/DIKW Pyramid, an important concept in the field of Knowledge Management.

We as a community of world citizens are faced with multiple simultaneous global crises. When attempting to resolve problems, it should be obvious that bullying, intimidating, showing lack of respect for one another and not respecting truth will only create obstacles to successfully resolving our mutual challenges. In order to successfully resolve our issues, it is important to go back to the basics and treat one another with respect and civility, focusing on common ground, using our heads as well as our hearts. It is my hope that the common ground and universal principles contained in this book can be a source of inspiration and wisdom during these times of great change.

In this Collector's Edition, I hope you enjoyed reading the heart essence of *The Rainbow Bridge*.

Contact Information

To order additional books or to contact the author:

Spirit Rising Productions
2261 Market Street, #637
San Francisco, CA 94114

Office: 415-462-1538
Web: www.spiritrising.tv
Email: Brent@SpiritRising.TV

Conscious Intentions

May you, all your relations and all beings everywhere be showered with love, compassion, wisdom, happiness, joy, peace, bliss, ecstasy, appreciation, dedication, devotion, commitment, abundance, prosperity and pleasure... now and in all times.

May peace, abundance and joy return to Earth.

Final Thoughts

Was this book too simple? Did it feel like it was just for beginners? Did it seem too elementary? If so, welcome to the crowd. And don't forget that *life is not always as it appears.*

It is not by chance that you are reading this book. Now that you have it in your hands, *keep it and read it again from time to time,* and don't be surprised if you start to see it in a different way each time you read it. Flip it open to a random page to see what message synchronistically appears... and remember it is not accidental.

Most of all, don't be surprised if you start to see yourself as a beautiful character in a dream who is waking up to the concept that *you are much more than the character you play in this dream of life...*